RAPTORS!

OWLS

Ethan Danielson

New York

Published in 2016 by The Rosen Publishing Group, Inc.
29 East 21st Street, New York, NY 10010

First Edition

Editor: Sarah Machajewski
Book Design: Mickey Harmon

Photo Credits: Cover series logo Elena Paletskaya/Shutterstock.com; cover, pp. 1, 3–4, 6, 8, 10, 12, 14, 16, 18, 20, 22–24 (border texture, fact box) Picsfive/Shutterstock.com; cover (background scene) karamysh/Shutterstock.com; cover (owl perched) LesPalenik/Shutterstock.com; cover (owl flying) Ondrej Prosicky/Shutterstock.com; p. 5 outdoorsman/Shutterstock.com; p. 7 Mikhail Kolesnikov/Shutterstock.com; p. 9 (inset) Mark Bridger/Shutterstock.com; p. 9 (main) Thanakorn Hongphan/Shutterstock.com; p. 11 (main) hutch photography/Shutterstock.com; p. 11 (snowy owl) Michael C. Gray/Shutterstock.com; p. 11 (burrowing owl) David Nagy/Shutterstock.com; p. 13 (inset) Michael Duva/Getty Images; p. 13 (main) Roger Eritja/Photographer's Choice/Getty Images; p. 15 (main) Mark Caunt/Shutterstock.com; p. 15 (inset) xavier gallego morell/Shutterstock.com; p. 17 rokopix/Shutterstock.com; p. 19 Johann Schumacher/Photolibrary/Getty Images; p. 21 BMJ/Shutterstock.com; p. 22 (owl flying) Jaroslaw Saternus/Shutterstock.com; p. 22 (owl head) Christian Schoissingeyer/Shutterstock.com.

Library of Congress Cataloging-in-Publication Data

Danielson, Ethan, 1956-
 Owls / Ethan Danielson.
    pages cm. — (Raptors!)
 Includes index.
 ISBN 978-1-5081-4272-0 (pbk.)
 ISBN 978-1-5081-4251-5 (6 pack)
 ISBN 978-1-5081-4252-2 (library binding)
 1. Owls—Juvenile literature. I. Title.
 QL696.S8D36 2015
 598.9′7—dc23
                                    2015034091

Manufactured in the United States of America

CPSIA Compliance Information: Batch #BW16PK: For Further Information contact Rosen Publishing, New York, New York at 1-800-237-9932

Contents

Who's That?

Owls have captured people's attention for thousands of years. It's easy to see why. Owls are mysterious creatures of the night. With excellent senses, they're also top hunters. They make almost no noise when they fly, and they observe silently from trees with their big, round eyes. Owls can turn their head almost completely around!

Who are these wonderful birds? There are many answers to this question, but one answer is simple. They're raptors.

The bird pictured here is a long-eared owl. This kind of owl is known for having ear feathers that stick up and out.

5

Meet the Raptor Family

You may be wondering what a raptor is. A raptor is a very **unique** kind of bird—of the 10,000 species, or kinds, of birds in the world, only a few of them can be called raptors.

All raptors have the following features in common. Raptors are birds of **prey**. Hunting is easy for raptors because their body is built for it. They have excellent eyesight, which helps them spot prey. Sharp **talons** help raptors catch food, and a sharp beak helps rip it apart.

RAPTOR FACTOR

The raptor family includes owls, vultures, buzzards, eagles, hawks, and falcons.

Raptors are carnivores, which means they eat only meat. Every part of their body, from their head to their feet, helps raptors hunt the food they need to survive.

All About Owls

Owls are raptors, but they also belong to a group of birds called Strigiformes. There are about 200 species in this group. These species are put into one of two families—true owls and barn owls.

What's the difference between true owls and barn owls? Barn owls are known for their heart-shaped face. Their feet are a little different than those of true owls. Besides that, there aren't many differences. In fact, scientists aren't even sure if owls should be **classified** this way. It may change in the future.

RAPTOR FACTOR

There are more owl species in the true owl family than in the barn owl family.

barn owl

true owl

True owl and barn owl species are nocturnal. That means they're mostly active at night and sleep during the day.

9

Where Do Owls Live?

Owls are found all over the world. They live on every continent except Antarctica. There are 19 species of owls in North America. They include the great horned owl, snowy owl, barn owl, burrowing owl, and screech owl.

Owls live in many kinds of **habitats**. They live in forests, mountains, and open plains. Some owls live in deserts, which are hot, dry areas. The snowy owl lives in cold, Arctic habitats. Owls also live in our neighborhoods.

RAPTOR FACTOR

There are probably several owl species that live near your home, but you may not know it since they're awake only when you're sleeping!

snowy owl

great horned owl

burrowing owl

Most owls nest in trees. Some nest on the ground, and
the burrowing owl nests in underground burrows.

Very Good Vision

Have you ever walked outside at night and seen a pair of glowing eyes staring at you? Don't be alarmed—it's probably an owl! Since owls are active at night, their eyes have **adapted** to see in the dark. Owl eyes are large and wide so they can take in as much light as possible.

Owls can't move their eyes—they can only stare forward. If owls want to look around, they have to turn their head. Luckily for owls, they can twist their head almost completely around.

> An owl's eyes both face in the same direction, like people's eyes. This gives them binocular vision, which means both eyes work together to create a single image. This helps them judge how big and far away something is.

13

Even Better Hearing

Owls hunt at night. In the dark, it's sometimes easier to hear prey than it is to see it. Owls have excellent hearing, which they use to locate prey.

Owls have an ear opening on each side of their head. The thousands of feathers that cover an owl's face help guide sounds to their ear holes. Each sound reaches the ear holes at a different angle. The owl's brain then puts the sounds together, figuring out exactly where the sound is coming from.

Most owls eat tiny **mammals**, such as mice, lemmings, gophers, and voles. They also eat snakes. These animals often hide in tall grass or under leaves or snow, but even this is no match for an owl's sharp hearing.

Silent Fliers

Owl prey moves quickly, so it's best for an owl if the prey can't hear it coming. Most owl species fly without making any noise. That's because they have feathers that are adapted for silent flight.

Most birds' feathers are stiff, so the air makes a "wooshing" noise as it travels over them. Not owls, though. Their feathers have soft edges. Air passes over the feathers without a sound. Silent flight makes owls **stealthy** predators. Their prey doesn't stand a chance when it can't **detect** danger coming.

RAPTOR FACTOR

Owls can't chew their food, so they rip off small pieces and swallow them whole. Later, they cough up pellets, which are lumps of bones and hair their body can't break down.

Owls have several advantages over the creatures they hunt. Their eyes detect the tiniest movements. They hear extremely soft sounds. They fly silently and under cover of darkness. Prey can run, it can hide, but it can't beat the **magnificent** owl.

Staying Hidden

Owls are as good at hiding as they are at staying silent. Their feathers provide excellent camouflage. Camouflage is an animal's natural coloring that helps it blend in with its surroundings.

The eastern screech owl nests in trees. Its brown, gray, and black feathers make it hard to tell if you're looking at tree bark or an owl. The snowy owl's white feathers are a perfect **disguise** against snow. Like these birds, other owl species survive in their habitats thanks to their camouflage.

RAPTOR FACTOR

Owls are top predators, but they're hunted, too. Camouflage keeps them hidden from cats, foxes, and bigger owls, which sometimes prey on baby owls.

Can you find the owl in this picture, or does its camouflage hide it too well?

"Hoots" There?

Owls may be silent when they hunt, but they otherwise make a lot of noise. In fact, you're more likely to hear an owl than see it. Its hoot, which is the name for an owl's call, lets you know an owl is nearby.

When you hear hooting, it's probably two owls calling to each other. Males and females respond to each other with different kinds of hoots to tell where they are. They also hoot to mark their territory. Each owl species has its own hoot.

RAPTOR FACTOR

Barn owls don't hoot—they screech.

Owls make all kinds of noises, including hooting, screaming, screeching, and more. Each sound means something different.

The Mysterious Owl

People have always taken an interest in owls. Maybe it's because of their mysterious nature. There's still a lot to learn about these striking birds.

Despite their cool features, amazing adaptations, and beautiful coloring, owls don't like to make themselves known. They prefer to live alone and be left alone.

Owls aren't easily seen, but that doesn't mean they can't see you. The next time you go out at night, look around. Can you tell if an owl is watching you?

Glossary

adapt: To change to better survive in a habitat. An adaptation is a change that helps an animal survive in its habitat.

classify: To assign something to a category based on shared qualities.

detect: To notice the presence of someone or something.

disguise: Something that keeps someone hidden from others.

habitat: The natural home of an animal or plant.

magnificent: Wonderful.

mammal: A warm-blooded animal that has a backbone and hair, and feeds milk to its young.

prey: An animal that's hunted by another animal for food. Also, to hunt and kill for food.

stealthy: Quiet and secretly.

talon: A bird's sharp claw.

unique: Special or different.

Index

Websites

Due to the changing nature of Internet links, PowerKids Press has developed an online list of websites related to the subject of this book. This site is updated regularly. Please use this link to access the list: www.powerkidslinks.com/rapt/owl